STARS OF HIP-HOP

NICKI MINAJ

MUSICIAN AND FASHION SUPERSTAR

LISA IDZIKOWSKI

Enslow Publishing
101 W. 23rd Street
Suite 240
New York, NY 10011
USA
enslow.com

Published in 2020 by Enslow Publishing, LLC.
101 W. 23rd Street, Suite 240, New York, NY 10011

Library of Congress Cataloging-in-Publication Data
Names: Idzikowski, Lisa, author.
Title: Nicki Minaj : musician and fashion superstar / Lisa Idzikowski.
Description: New York : Enslow Publishing, [2020] | Series: Stars of hip-hop |
Audience: 2 | Includes bibliographical references and index.
Identifiers: LCCN 2018050380 | ISBN 9781978509610 (library bound) | ISBN
9781978510401 (pbk.) | ISBN 9781978510425 (6 pack)
Subjects: LCSH: Minaj, Nicki—Juvenile literature. | Rap musicians—United
States—Juvenile literature.
Classification: LCC ML3930.M313 I48 2019 | DDC 782.42164092 [B] —dc23
LC record available at https://lccn.loc.gov/2018050380

Printed in the United States of America

To Our Readers: We have done our best to make sure all websites in this book were
active and appropriate when we went to press. However, the author and the publisher
have no control over and assume no liability for the material available on those
websites or on any websites they may link to. Any comments or suggestions can be
sent by email to customerservice@enslow.com.

Photo Credits: Cover, p. 1 Johnny Nunez/WireImage/Getty Images; p. 5 Leon
Bennett/WireImage/Getty Images; p. 7 Jason LaVeris/FilmMagic/Getty Images;
pp. 8, 18, 24, 26 Kevin Mazur/WireImage/Getty Images; p. 11 EQRoy/Shutterstock
.com; p. 13 Kevin Winter/Getty Images; p. 14 Michael Caulfield/Getty Images; p. 17
Dimitrios Kambouris/Getty Images; p. 20 Jamie McCarthy/WireImage/Getty Images;
p. 23 Jason LaVeris/FilmMagic/Getty Images.

CONTENTS

NICKI'S START

Nicki Minaj is a famous hip-hop star. Some say she is the greatest female **rapper** of all time. Her real name is Onika Tanya Maraj. She was born on December 8, 1982, in Trinidad. Trinidad is an island. It was home for Nicki and her parents, Robert and Carol. It was home for many other family members, too. But her parents moved away when she was very little. They went to the United States.

Nicki Minaj is excited to attend the 2015 BET Awards in Los Angeles, California.

Nicki's parents were looking for better jobs and a better life. Nicki couldn't go along. Instead she stayed with her grandmother. But she had one big wish. And it came true when she was five years old.

NICKI'S NEW HOME

Nicki's mother and father sent for her! It was time to move to her new home. She said goodbye to her friends and family in Trinidad. Nicki was happy to be with her parents again. But her happiness did not last.

There was not much to like about New York City for Nicki. It was cold. Her house was small. It was in a bad neighborhood. People sold drugs on the streets.

"I think before I could remember wanting to do anything else, I knew that I wanted to be in charge."[1]

Big troubles started. Her father lost his job. He started drinking alcohol to deal with his problems. He also began using

Nicki Minaj and her mother, Carol Maraj, pose together at the BET Awards show.

drugs a lot. Her parents screamed and fought all the time. Nicki hated all the problems at home. Her father took things from their house. He sold some of their furniture to buy drugs.

NICKI'S FIRST RAP

Nicki's father got mad all the time. He punched holes in the walls. One night, he even set their house on fire! Nicki wasn't at home that night. Luckily, her

Nicki Minaj sings to the crowd in a flashy costume during the iHeartRadio Music Festival in 2011.

Nicki's Many Characters

Nicki pretends to be different characters in her songs. This started when she was a young girl with her first character, "Cookie." Her characters include a Barbie, a ninja, and others.

mother wasn't hurt. But Nicki lost all her toys and clothes. And she also lost all her memories.

How did Nicki deal with it? She loved to sing and write. She loved to read. Nicki also liked to dress up and play pretend. And when she was eleven, she wrote her first **rap**. It was about a girl named "Cookie."

THE RIGHT SCHOOL FOR NICKI

Nicki Minaj has said, "Acting was my first thing."[1] She might say that her career started in high school. The Fiorello H. LaGuardia High School of Music & Art and Performing Arts in New York was a special place. Kids who wanted to sing, dance, and act went there. Nicki's mother knew it was the right high school for her daughter.

"That school changed my life . . . [E]veryone was able to express themselves."[2]

This is a look at Nicki Minaj's high school today.

At first, Nicki was turned down. Her singing tryout didn't go well. But her mother wouldn't let her give up. Nicki tried again. This time she landed a spot in the program for acting. At first Nicki was scared. But she knew that it was the right place for her.

A PERFECT FIT

Nicki worried about going to a new school. Would she make new friends? Would people like her? Yes. She fit right in. Everyone was creative. The school didn't have a **dress code**. Kids dressed exactly the way they wanted. Nicki also had a boyfriend. For a while, she was more interested in him than in school. She skipped classes. Luckily, she took extra classes and graduated.

Great Grads

Many famous entertainers went to Nicki's high school. Actors Jennifer Aniston and Ansel Elgort graduated from there. Fellow rappers Azealia Banks and Awkwafina did, too.

Nicki Minaj performs at a 2011 Staples Center show. Her colorful style started in high school.

OFF INTO THE WORLD

By the end of high school, **talent scouts** showed interest in Nicki. They thought she had good acting skills. Nicki thought it was

At a 2010 concert in California, Nicki Minaj sings to the US military. Music was the key to her happiness.

her ticket to stardom. But not so fast. She really wanted to live on her own. And that meant having to pay for everything. None of the talent scouts offered her steady work. So she found jobs for herself.

At first, she tried work as a waitress. Later, she worked in an office. Nicki hated both jobs. She realized that only one thing would make her truly happy. She had to make it big in the world of music.

NICKI'S RISE TO FAME

Nicki Minaj dove into music. She wrote lyrics. She listened to all kinds of popular music. She sang to anyone who would listen. It wasn't easy. But she never gave up. She worked and worked. She just had to be a big hit.

A friend asked Minaj to help him with some music. She wrote parts of his song. He loved her work. That did it! Minaj was going to make herself the best female **emcee**, or rapper.

Nicki Minaj and her mother, Carol, go to a 2018 New York fashion show. Her mother has always been the most important person in her life.

She had one big goal in the back of her mind. It kept her going. She wanted to be able to take care of her mother. But she had to be rich to do that.

Nicki Minaj, Jay-Z, and Kanye West perform to a crowd in Yankee Stadium in 2010.

GETTING SOCIAL

Things came together for Minaj. She put her music and photographs up on a site called **MySpace**. Her wild style made her stand out. People found her. They liked what they saw. She soon had lots of fans.

Minaj got noticed by other rappers, too. She worked with the famous rapper Lil Wayne. She joined his record label. It is called Young Money Entertainment. Before long, she had recorded three **mixtapes**. Her third was called *Beam Me Up Scotty*. News about her music took off. Minaj was a guest singer on the songs of other stars, such as Kanye West. The song they did together is called "Monster."

What's in a Name?

In the music world, many performers have given names to their fans. Many of Nicki Minaj's fans are girls. She calls them her Barbies, Barbs, and Barbz.

THE TIME WAS RIGHT

Nicki Minaj's fame grew and grew. Her single **track** "Your Love" made it onto the Billboard Hot 100 chart. This is a list of the most popular songs in America. Her "Barbies" eagerly waited to hear her next song. The time

Nicki Minaj gets ready to sell her lipstick on November 23, 2010. It is called "Pink Friday" after her album.

was right for her next big move. Her first **studio** album, *Pink Friday,* came out. It

"I would go into my room and kneel down at the foot of my bed and pray that God would make me rich so that I could take care of my mother."[1]

soared to the top of the music charts. And it sold one million copies in a month!

But some people didn't like the new sound. A few music critics even complained that the songs were not Nicki Minaj. They said she had moved away from rap. They thought she wanted to change over to **pop** instead. Minaj didn't pay attention to them.

NICKI GIVES BACK

It was time for Nicki Minaj to give back. She liked dolls as a young girl. She even pretended to be one. A toy company wanted to make a Barbie doll that looked just like her. The doll would be sold. The money would help other people. It would buy food for people dealing with HIV and AIDS.

Minaj also sent aid to India. Several villages received help. Her money

Nicki Minaj shows off her Barbie necklace at a 2011 National Basketball Players Association party. She teamed up with the makers of Barbie to help others.

built new water wells. Now these areas have clean water. The villages also got computers, thanks to the rapper.

Nicki Minaj autographs a photo for a young fan in 2012.

NICKI SAYS STAY IN SCHOOL

Minaj feels that she has been lucky. She is a top singer. She has her own perfume, lipstick, nail polish, and clothing lines. But she also said, "My happiness doesn't come from money or fame. My happiness comes from seeing life without struggle."[1] Minaj believes in schooling. She tells fans to go to school every day. Nothing is more important for their future.

And she is doing something to prove it! Minaj has surprised some of her fans. She paid some of their college costs.

> "My happiness doesn't come from money or fame. My happiness comes from seeing life without struggle."

Later on, she started a **scholarship fund**. And that helps even more of her fans go to school.

NICKI THE QUEEN

Onika Tanya Maraj has come far. As a little girl, she was scared. She grew up and wanted

At the 2015 "Shining A Light" benefit concert, Nicki Minaj recites a poem by the famous poet Maya Angelou. Minaj's own words have also reached people around the world.

Nicki the Actress

Nicki Minaj isn't just a top musical performer. She acts, too. She has appeared in a commercial for Pepsi. Her voice is also in the movie *Ice Age: Continental Drift*.

to be the best rapper. Now she is Nicki Minaj, the "Queen of Queens." She is a proud rapper, singer, and songwriter. She has recorded four studio albums. And she has many fans.

But being famous is not the only important thing in Minaj's life. She helps others. She also visits her old neighborhoods. People love to see her there. Minaj is good to friends and is happy to take care of her family.

TIMELINE

1982 Nicki Minaj is born on December 8 in Port of Spain, Trinidad.

1987 Minaj moves to New York to be with her parents.

1993 Minaj writes her first rap at age eleven.

2000 Minaj graduates from LaGuardia High School of Music & Art and Performing Arts.

2007 Minaj records first mixtape, *Playtime Is Over*.

2009 Minaj performs with Lil Wayne as a special guest star.

2010 She releases her first studio album, *Pink Friday*, in November.

2010 She has more singles on the Hot 100 Billboard Chart than any other artist.

2011 Toy company Mattel creates a Nicki Minaj Barbie doll to be sold for charity.

2012 Minaj becomes the most followed hip-hop star on Twitter.

2012 She releases her second studio album, *Pink Friday: Roman Reloaded,* in April.

2014 Minaj's third album, *The Pinkprint,* comes out in December.

2017 Minaj gives some lucky fans money to pay for school.

2018 Minaj sets up the Student of the Game scholarship to help fans pay for college.

2018 Minaj releases her fourth album, *Queen*, in August.

CHAPTER NOTES

CHAPTER 1. NICKI'S START

1. Ryan Roschke, "Nicki Minaj Spits Wisdom as Flawlessly as She Does Rhymes," Popsugar, April 24, 2016, https://www.popsugar.com/celebrity/Nicki-Minaj-Interview-Time-April-2016-41027427.

CHAPTER 2. THE RIGHT SCHOOL FOR NICKI

1. Ray Rahman, "Nicki Minaj on Her First Movie Role," *Entertainment Weekly,* July 13, 2012, https://ew.com/article/2012/07/13/nicki-minaj-her-first-movie-role/.

2. Jonah Weiner, "'I'm a Vulnerable Woman and I'm Proud of That' - Nicki Minaj," Independent.ie, March 16, 2015, https://www.independent.ie/entertainment/music/im-a-vulnerable-woman-and-im-proud-of-that-nicki-minaj-31048953.html.

CHAPTER 3. NICKI'S RISE TO FAME

1. Brian Hiatt, "Nicki Minaj: The New Queen of Hip-Hop," *Rolling Stone,* December 9, 2010, https://www.rollingstone.com/music/music-news/nicki-minaj-the-new-queen-of-hip-hop-103304/.

CHAPTER 4. NICKI GIVES BACK

1. Nicki Minaj (@nikiyminaj), "My happiness doesn't come from money or fame. My happiness comes from seeing life without struggle," Twitter, June 14, 2015, 7:00 p.m. https://twitter.com/nikiyminaj/status/610265534207135744.

WORDS TO KNOW

dress code A set of rules that tell students what they can and cannot wear.

emcee A rapper or a person who controls the microphone, also written as MC.

mixtape A collection of songs that an artist puts out without the help of a recording studio.

MySpace A social media website.

pop A type of music, short for "popular."

rap A type of music where words are spoken, usually fast, instead of sung.

rapper A musical artist that raps.

scholarship fund Money to help students pay for school.

studio A special room used to record music.

talent scout A person who searches for the next big star.

track An individual piece of music recorded on an album or mixtape.

LEARN MORE

BOOKS

Earl, C. F. *Nicki Minaj*. Vestal, NY: Village Earth Press, 2016.

Mattern, Joanne. *Nicki Minaj*. Hockessin, DE: Mitchell Lane Publishers, 2014.

Morse, Eric. *What Is Hip-Hop?* Brooklyn, NY: Akashic Books, 2017.

WEBSITES

Billboard: Nicki Minaj
www.billboard.com/music/nicki-minaj
Explore Nicki Minaj's chart history, watch videos, and catch up on news about her.

Kidzworld: Nicki Minaj Bio
www.kidzworld.com/article/25272-nicki-minaj-bio
Find out more about Nicki Minaj.

INDEX